Lightning In A Bottle

3 Easy Rules For Writing More Profitable Radio Commercials

Blaine Parker

ISBN: 0-9963052-1-1
ISBN-13: 978-0-9963052-1-1

DEDICATION

To Dave, Terry, Dave, Bob, the courageous clients, and everyone else who put up with me while working to make better radio for small-business advertisers across the country.

WARNING: If you've ever worked with me, read any of my books or blog posts or articles, or have heard me speak from the stage, much of this is going to sound familiar. And even if you feel as if you've heard it before, you may still find it useful. Possibly even enjoyable. Especially if you didn't follow any of it the first time.

CONTENTS

ACKNOWLEDGMENTS

No project such as this ever happens in a vacuum. Were it not for my collaborators in radio, and the clients who had the courage to move forward despite feeling the fear of sailing into (for them) uncharted waters, none of this would have been possible. There are more of you than one can possibly thank by name. You all know who you are. Additionally, were it not for my boss at Slow Burn Marketing, our President For Life, the Fabulous Honey Parker, this meager tome would look like it had been art directed by a radio producer. Thank you all for playing.

BLAINE PARKER

A MODEST FOREWORD

Lightning is powerful.

A lightning bolt lasts only about 2/10 of a second.

Like lightning, great radio creative is powerful.

Great copy will produce results on virtually any radio station. It's not about being on the most listened-to station in the market that will produce results for the advertiser; it's the radio message itself that will make the difference. (I know. I've lived this. After managing radio stations for over 30 years, working with hundreds of businesses to create effective radio advertising, I'm now teaching these skills to the next generation.)

This book is much like its namesake: a lightning fast read, powerful and illuminating.

Wasting not a word, Blaine Parker relays three secrets of successful radio advertising that have taken me—and most of my colleagues—a lifetime to acquire.

Used correctly, words are the most powerful force man commands.

Anyone who wants to grow Return On Investment will find this modest book a *must* read, and a book that they will want to keep close by to always remind them of three principles of creating radio commercials that are electric.

Dick Taylor, CRMC/CDMC
Broadcast Professor
Western Kentucky University
School of Journalism & Broadcasting
Bowling Green, Kentucky

WHO ARE YOU AND WHY ARE YOU HERE?

Are you looking for a comprehensive guide to creating wildly successful radio advertising?

I readily and cheerfully admit: This is not it.

If you continue reading expecting such a guide, you will be sorely disappointed.

However, do you work in radio and feel that somehow, you're missing some secret? Or, are you a small business owner who's tried (unsuccessfully) to advertise your business on air? Then this tiny tome might just be for you.

There's a simple reality in our world: all of us are salesmen of some kind. Maybe you actually wear the salesman hat. Maybe you sell in your own business. Perhaps you're doing marketing for yourself or others. Whoever you are and whatever you do, you sell for a living.

Most of us do.

What you may not be is a writer. And the last thing a non-writer wants to hear about is how to write. But really, this is not a writing how-to guide.

Instead, we're going to talk about something that should be near and dear to the heart of every salesman: simple, effective strategy and tactics.

Specifically, this is about three simple steps for making more effective radio commercials.

WHAT IS THIS BOOK AND WHY IS IT HERE?

This is a modest book.

For a moment, calling it a "booklet" almost seemed more accurate. But then, a booklet is also a pamphlet. And at roughly 12,000 words, that too seemed inaccurate. Plus, in digital form, can one really have an "e-booklet" or "e-pamphlet"? I have no idea.

We could have called this an "information product." But then, that comes with all other kinds of associated baggage.

So, "modest book" it is.

This book was born several years ago during my work as an advertising creative director at a national radio network.

Back then, one of the worst possible ways any account rep could ever introduce me to a new advertiser was as "our national award-winning copywriter."

It was always a cringe-worthy moment.

Yes, there have been awards. Many, in fact. Some were really huge, impressive awards with big, heavy trophies and even enormous cash prizes.

So, what?

To a business owner advertising on radio, those trophies and cash prizes are irrelevant. The advertiser doesn't give a flying rat's ass about my advertising awards.

The advertiser is there to get results.

He's preparing to invest in radio advertising and wants a return on that investment.

Awards are about me.

ROI is about him.

All that said, I also enjoyed a reputation as a fixer.

Frequently, an account rep would come to me with a radio commercial that simply wasn't functioning. It was running on air and not producing results. What was the problem? And what could be done to make it better?

Eventually, after providing so much cure, it seemed like a good idea to offer a few ounces of prevention. Try to nip at least some of those problem commercials in the bud. Working with various radio stations from New York to California (not to mention the national network), there were far too many account reps for me to be helping each one of them individually.

But what if I could put together a presentation illustrative of how we in the creative department analyze commercials that aren't working? What if this presentation had examples of how we as copywriters look at an underperforming message, and how we analyze it in an effort to fix it?

Radio account reps often do not consider themselves writers. Radio account reps are also often stuck writing their own commercials. Often, the advertisers help them. They work together in a vacuum—often as newbies in the world of radio, which makes things even more challenging. If it were possible to show them examples of better ways to think about the on-air sell, maybe it would mitigate the need for fixing underperforming advertising.

Lightning In A Bottle was born.

That was in the early 21st century. The phrase itself was born much earlier. The concept of "lightning in a bottle" was born in the 19th century.

It's a literal reference to Benjamin Franklin's efforts to capture electricity in a jar.

Over the decades, "lightning in a bottle" has evolved to various different meanings. But here, in the case of this modest little book, we're speaking metaphorically about the containment of energy—specifically the potential energy of a 60-second radio container (a commercial) to ignite interest in the listener and make them take action.

Lightning In A Bottle was originally a 40-minute oral presentation. Sometimes, the presentation was made live. Other times, a recording was played for account reps at a sales meeting. The response was always positive.

But the thing that always surprised me was when, years after the fact, long after I'd left the network, some sales manager would contact me and ask about it—specifically whether I had "anything else like that."

Obviously, this modest effort at making things better from the start had struck a nerve with people. And now, more than a decade after it originally debuted, it seemed like a good idea to make it available more widely.

So here it is.

And again, this is not a comprehensive guide to creating radio advertising.

Instead, this is a cursory effort to demonstrate to the overworked professional with a short attention span a few examples of how to make their radio commercials better.

Also, in order to beef up the "why" behind the how, this book contains some basic background and procedural material that wasn't part of the original presentation.

And one important note: all of the advertisers' names (along with phone numbers and locations) have been changed. Otherwise, the ad copy presented here represents what went on the air.

All of it is real.

None of it is award-winning.

And none of it is supposed to represent anything like genius advertising.

Instead, it is intended to represent competent advertising copy. This is the kind of copy almost anyone working at a radio station can create as long as they have an understanding of the customer, the medium, and the sales process. And, an understanding of how to listen and how to put words on paper.

With that, let's look at capturing us some lightning.

WHAT TO EXPECT...

Want to talk about your feelings?

Of course not.

But the first thing we're going to cover is emotion. No discussion of effective radio advertising is complete without addressing emotion.

Next, we'll talk about a few simple, technical details of radio advertising best practices.

Then, we'll look at The Three Rules that you didn't even know you came here to find. They are, in order:

1. No Swiss Army Knives
2. Propose Marriage With A Diamond
3. Don't Be Clever

Finally, we'll recap. And say all of this all over again.

And with any luck, you'll walk away from this lean, mean little volume with a slightly better ability to turn local radio advertising into a magnetic money machine.

EMOTION
(AND WHY YOU SHOULD FEEL LIKE YOU CARE)

Every single person who has ever entered professional sales at any level in any place has likely heard this old chestnut: "Sales decisions are made emotionally and justified intellectually."

What does that even mean?

Here's the nugget of information that is lacking when that arthritic old horse gets trotted out: The success of simple daily existence is based on emotional decisions.

Without emotions, human beings are incapable of making decisions.

This has been demonstrated repeatedly, and by accident. When individuals suffer damage to an area of the brain governing emotion, they can become incapable of making even simple decisions. Their lives go off the rails.

Let's get vaguely and irresponsibly geeky for just a moment. (I'm no doctor, nor have I played one on the radio, but bear with me.) We're talking about damage to the orbitofrontal cortex and the amygdala.

Your orbitofrontal cortex is part of the prefrontal cortex.

Scientists believe it's all about emotion and reward in decision making.

As for the amygdala, the word is Greek for "almond." You have two almond-shaped amygdalae deep in your brain. They've been shown to process memory, decision-making, and emotional reactions.

You might be an otherwise responsible, hard-working individual right now. But, damage your amygdala and/or orbitofrontal cortex, and your life becomes a hell. You can't run your own life in any way that makes sense. Without your emotional governors, you lose your power to make intelligent decisions.

All this to say: decisions are by default an emotional process.

As this applies to advertising, the most effective sales messages are crafted with an understanding of emotional reactions to even the smallest details.

That bears repeating.

The most effective sales messages are crafted with an understanding of emotional reactions to even the smallest details.

Especially in the context of radio, even single words matter.

That cannot be stressed enough.

Even. Single. Words. Matter.

Once, someone sent me a commercial for a mortgage broker. He asked, "What's wrong with this? It's not generating any calls."

I listened to the commercial. It started out fine. The mortgage broker was voicing the message, and doing so very credibly.

The sales message was being told as a story, which is good. Human beings are wired for stories. We will automatically tune in to anything that smacks of "Once upon a time…"

The conflict in the story was this: a single mother with three children was having trouble financing her home.

OK. It speaks to solving a problem for the prospect.

But then…

"The mother had cancer."

You hear that screeching sound? That's the wheels on the sales message coming to a dead stop and falling off.

When you're trying to sell someone on the better reality of home finance with you, and you introduce The Single Mother With Cancer, the sales pitch is over.

You have suddenly overshadowed the potential joy of a 30-year fixed at 3.7 percent with the looming specter of death and orphans.

The emotional charge of cancer trumps the emotional charge of the mortgage broker's better reality for the customer.

Emotion is key.

But emotional content also requires relevance.

There's a reason that the airwaves are filled with advertising for health supplements: this is a category where deft hucksters have figured out how to tap into the emotions in a way that sells bottles of pills.

Figure out your prospect's emotional buttons *vis à vis* the product or service, and understand how to push them.

Now, there's another old chestnut that always gets rolled out for radio advertising.: "Radio is an emotional medium."

Which is true.

Of any media used skillfully, radio is the most emotionally evocative. That's because it plays to that enormous movie screen in our heads.

Radio can make us imagine so much.

It can engage us so thoroughly.

One reason it's such a popular medium for the political talk format is it's easy to polarize the listeners. It's easy to make them love you or hate you.

One problem with learning that "radio is an emotional medium" is that the "logical" conclusion for many becomes, "We need to do funny commercials!"

Because people love "funny" commercials. Right? Because "funny" evokes laughter. And laughter is an emotion. And if we make people laugh, they feel emotion and buy. Right?

Wrong.

Laughter is not emotion.

Laughter is merely an outward display of emotion.

The emotion itself can be one of several. If you're going to make people laugh, they need to laugh for the right reason.

"Funny" by itself is not a sales trigger. If you're going to make someone laugh, it better be about the right thing. And that right thing better be linked to delivering a better reality by using the advertiser's product or service.

Some advertising professionals love to cling to a partial truth: advertising great David Ogilvy hated funny advertising, saying that people will not buy from a clown. Bear in mind that Ogilvy also said, "The best ideas come as jokes. Make your thinking as funny as possible." So obviously, he wasn't anti-comedy. But he was very much pro-relevance. And too often, comedy in advertising isn't relevant to the sales message.

Getting a laugh doesn't necessarily get the sale. More likely to result in a sale is getting a prospect to smile. Because smiles are more often linked to humor rather than comedy. Comedy engages the head, elicits surprise, and creates a big laugh. Humor goes deeper. Humor engages the heart.

A great example of the power of humor is the last 30 years (as of this writing) of radio commercials from Motel 6. Tom Bodett's folksy, regular-guy voice, along with the folksy guitar and fiddle of Tom Faulkner and Milo Deering, are a perfect illustration of how humor is evocative and enduring. Comedy, by contrast, elicits a quick and surprising laugh; it dissipates, and typically leaves the listener without any emotional resonance.

All this to say: To be effective, advertising has to hit the right emotional button.

We don't want to hit irrelevant emotional buttons. They create distractions and send people away–not unlike the button connected to "cancer" when you're trying to sell the joy of better home finance.

Yes, it's OK to be funny.

But it's not OK to be funny at the expense of the sell.

It's paramount to be emotionally evocative in a relevant and resonant manner.

To borrow from a famous quote by the renowned Canadian neuroscientist Dr. Donald Calne, "intellect leads to conclusions," but "emotions lead to action."

We want action.

We want the action of deciding to buy. That decision is controlled by the emotional brain.

After the sale, the buyer will rationalize the purchase. But we still need to get that buyer to the table. And dangling an emotionally relevant carrot is the way to do that.

Bottom Line: Capturing lightning in a bottle requires deft use of emotional content.

DETAILS, DETAILS

This is a quick overview of a few simple details that can also make or break a radio commercial's viability.

THE OFFER

One of the first things is The Offer. We have to offer something to the prospect.

In the classic, direct-response advertising mindset, the offer takes the form of "buy this now, and get this added value" or some version of that. Two for one. Half off the second one. Free today only. Those are easy-to-understand offers.

But that isn't the only kind of offer.

Here now, I become a heretic among the hardcore direct-response crowd.

A skillfully written commercial that offers a better reality can get away without saying something classically defined as an offer.

This heresy is what I call the "Intrinsic Offer."

It's possible to create highly effective radio commercials that offer a reality so vivid and so much better than everything else that's out there that there's no need to state a two-for-one/free-estimate/buy-now offer.

The wolves of direct response advertising hate that.

Again, going back to Motel 6. The intrinsic offer of Motel 6 is a clean, basic room with a phone and a TV for the lowest price of any national chain.

Almost nobody can tell you that much.

Because for most people, the offer is "We'll leave the light on for you." Some folks even think Tom Bodett owns Motel 6. (He doesn't. He's merely a performer.) This illustrates the emotional power of a truly evocative spot.

Flooded with phone calls.

Working with a local transmission repair service, I once wrote advertising that was so evocative, the place was flooded with phone calls—despite the fact there was no offer and no phone number.

There was no phone number because there really wasn't any reason for a phone number.

And the emotional charge came from the disarming idea that the owner of the shop was so utterly boring and fixated on transmissions that the only thing he could possibly do well was make your transmission run like new. (Yes, the message made fun of the advertiser and people loved it.)

Let's face it: people hate the whole idea of transmission repair. So, by linking the business name to powerful emotions, the offer of better transmission repair was so strong that the business name was all the listener needed.

The core customer was smart enough to dial 411 and say "Give me Rudy's Tranny Shop in Anonytown." (Not the real business name. Not a real city name.)

And yes, no phone number is anathema to the DR hounds. So be it. A powerful intrinsic offer from an easy-to-find business can make the phone number unnecessary.

THE CALL TO ACTION

After the offer comes The Call To Action.

Another misunderstood term, The Call To Action is not the same as The Offer.

The call to action is "call now," or "go online," or some other directive to act. It can even be, "Come see us at...."

If the message requires a classic offer and a call to action, PLEASE: put the call to action *after* the offer, NOT *before* the offer.

The construction of an offer and call to action should always be a step-by-step procedure.

If you want this, do this.

"Want half off? Call now."

And then comes the phone number.

DO NOT say, "Call 555-1212 to get half off."

Direct response radio advertising is a delicate thing, and requires very specific constructions in order to work. As a listener, the phone number or URL does me no good until I know what it's for.

THE URGENCY

This is another favorite of the direct response crowd. "Supplies are limited!" "This offer expires at midnight tonight!" "We may never make this offer again!"

Yes, it's often fabricated, artificial urgency.

It also sells. (See also: P.T. Barnum.)

I'm not exhorting you to be a huckster. We don't want to load down our messages with DR BS. Have some class. But where appropriate, go ahead and say that something is available in limited quantity. It doesn't hurt, and it can often help get the prospect off the couch.

NOW, LET'S TALK ABOUT MY NEEDS.

My need is for all copywriters everywhere to expunge the word "needs" from their vocabulary.

Motel 6 has never said, "For all your cheap-lodging needs."

Miller has never said, "For all your cold-beer needs."

Target has never said, "For all your well-designed, cheaply-made, making-you-feel-better-than-if-you-were-shopping-at-Walmart, crappy-product needs."

Motel 6 leaves the light on for you.

Miller gives you the champagne of beers.

Target makes you feel hipper than the people of Walmart.

In their day-to-day conversations, nobody ever says, "I have FILL IN THE BLANK needs."

They have wants and wishes and desires and maybe even requirements. It's up to you (as an advertiser) to fulfill them.

"Needs" is a word used by lazy-thinking copywriters, and obnoxious girlfriends who admonish, "You're not responsive to my needs!"

"Needs" puts up a barrier between the message and the listener.

If you are writing copy and use the word "needs," you haven't come close to understanding what you're selling, how you're selling it, or to whom it's being sold.

This also goes for jargon and techno-speak. And especially lazy-thinker ad-speak like, "There's never been a better time to buy," "our friendly, knowledgeable staff," "our 30,000-square-foot showroom," "it's our people that make the difference," "where the customer comes first," or any other bullshit (yes, I said "bullshit") that's constantly belched out by writers too lazy or afraid to turn an original phrase.

Dig deeper.

Yes, it's work. But the rewards are immense.

Bottom Line: In direct response especially, capturing lightning requires attention to the details—or the energy dissipates.

HERE NOW: THE THREE RULES

RULE 1

NO SWISS ARMY KNIVES—THROW A DART

You know the Swiss Army knife. It has a dozen different tools. Open up every tool in a Swiss Army knife and you know what happens?

That knife is useless—especially if you need to throw it at a target.

You cannot effectively wield a pocket knife bristling with open blades and a can opener and a file and a screwdriver and a saw blade and a corkscrew…

If you aim at a target and throw that knife, the knife will bounce off.

However, think about the humble dart.

A dart is a specialty tool.

It has one point and one purpose.

A dart is designed for aiming and throwing with intent, piercing its target and sticking there.

We want our advertising to be a dart.

We want a sharp pointy end to stick right in the target—which can be a problem if we don't happen know who the target is.

Without a well-defined target customer, it's much more difficult to have an effective ad.

Without a target we're hitting nothing, because we're flailing around in the dark with a knife blade, a corkscrew, a saw, a nail file, and an ivory toothpick.

When we target a specific customer, we can talk about that customer's specific situation and offer that specific person a specific better reality.

In other words, advertising is problem solving. And if a good advertisement really is a solution to a problem, we have to identify the person and the problem.

MESSING ABOUT IN BOATS

True story: I was given a commercial that wasn't working. Here's the Swiss Army knife that I listened to:

> ANNCR: Are you planning an event, your wedding or other celebration? Perhaps a church group or corporate event? Would you like to make your event, well, an *event*? Then have it aboard one of the beautiful dream-fleet yachts from Sea Ventures. For about what you'd pay to use a hotel, your gathering from 2 to 750 can go from the mundane to the memorable on a Sea Ventures yacht. Let God paint the backdrop for your wedding day. Have the wave-less waters of Nameless Harbor host your church or corporate event all for about what four walls and no view would cost you at a hotel. Get more information on your Sea Venture by calling 800-555-1212. That's 800-555-1212, or better yet, sail for yourself as this radio station hosts an onboard open house on September 13. See the dream fleet complete with free gondola rides, food, and a chance to win your own Sea Venture. Get more information by calling Sea

Venture Yacht Charters at 800-555-1212. That's 800-555-1212. That's Sea Venture, 800-555-1212.

Oh, my. Weddings *AND* corporate events? Yay! The most important day of my daughter's life can be every bit as romantic as the annual company booze cruise!

Let's face it, this message is not talking to any one person on any level that truly matters. It's all clinical, all bullet points, all generic. "Your gathering from 2 to 750"? That's the difference between a romantic dinner and a cattle drive. There is no focus on anything. There is zero emotion. And the Swiss Army knife blades are all open and waving in the air.

To be effective, a radio commercial must focus on one thing and one thing only. This commercial is talking about (a) your generic event, (b) your wedding, (c) your other celebration, (d) your church group (e) your corporate event and (f) the advertiser's open house.

In other words, this message focuses on nothing.

When was the last time you said, "Gee, I wonder where I should hold my other celebration?"

You never have. Guaranteed.

Each of these events is a unique undertaking with different demands and different emotions involved.

First, we need a target. It could be the corporate event, where the planner is trying to impress the boss who's trying to impress his clients. There are all kinds of emotions tied up in that, including fear and ego. But who's really the easiest target here? To his credit, the account rep who'd written the original copy knew that we needed a better, more targeted strategy. He's the one who began to focus, this time on weddings. We took it a step further.

We opened up the velvet-lined walnut box and took out the wedding dart.

That dart was aimed right at the bride's father.

Your daughter's getting married. Who are you and what matters to you? If you're her father, you worry about the cost, your daughter's happiness, and yes, even your vanity. You want people to remember this wedding for all the right reasons, how beautiful it was, how much fun they had and how expensive it must have been. (Yes, daddy has an ego, too.)

Take that wedding dart, and throw it right at dad's heart. And please, please, please—SHOW us some of that cruise. It's radio. Paint a picture of what this day might look like…

> MAN: (QUIETLY, WITH A RESTRAINED SMILE) The salt air is as sweet as nectar. Sunlight glistens like scattered jewels across Nameless Harbor. The guests laugh and dance as your boat slips past historical homes and famous yachts. Oh, and the bride! You never thought she could look even more stunning, but she does. To think you were going to use a mere hotel, a banquet room, four dead walls. Look, the same price, half the effort and you've got the sea, the sun, the moon and the stars with harbor seals frolicking in your wake. And tonight, the bride and the groom are departing in a Venetian gondola. They're all going to talk about this day for a long time.
>
> ANNCR: Sea Ventures! Charter a luxury yacht for the wedding of a lifetime. Dates for weddings and receptions are filling quickly, so call now for a free brochure, or to arrange a tour of the Sea Ventures luxury fleet. 1-800-555-1212. That's 1-800-555-1212. Sea Ventures Yacht Charters, transporting you from event…to adventure.

A little more interesting than the first one? Yep. And maybe a little corny. But how about more effective? During the time this commercial ran on one station, it outperformed all of the advertiser's other advertising media—*combined.*

And did you notice the believable urgency? "Dates are filling quickly." Uh-oh. I better hurry.

If we're not throwing a dart, we're not advertising to anybody.

FINANCE ME!

Another example of dart throwing: a new mortgage-broker advertiser. This is a small company with big ambitions. Never advertised on radio before.

So, consider for a second what most mortgage advertising on the radio sounds like. "Low rates! No points! No fees! No closing costs! Nothing added to your loan balance! Low rates! We'll even let you borrow our expensive pen when you sign the papers! Low rates! Call now!"

There isn't even a Swiss Army knife in that kind of ad. That's just waving in the air completely unarmed.

Well, this new advertiser understood the dart. We said, "Jack, you have to define your target borrower. If there was only one mortgage borrower left standing on the planet, what would he look like and what could you do for him?"

He told us exactly to whom he wanted to speak.

He told us how he could help that person. We gave him a dart to hit that target…

> ANNCR: Got $1,500 dollars cash? Is your credit score at least 600? You can buy a house now. Here's John Fantone of Mortgage Central.
>
> JOHN: At Mortgage Central, we're more than just

mortgage brokers. Mortgage Central is the center for homeowner success. We work with folks who thought home ownership was only for other people. Even if you've been through bankruptcy, call us for a free own-versus-rent analysis. If you've got $1,500 dollars cash and a credit score of at least 600, we'll run the numbers. Then we'll see what you can afford, and that can be as much as $300,000 with a zero down payment financed in as little as four days. If you think owning a home is for other people, call us for a second opinion.

ANNCR: Call Mortgage Central today. Ask for your free own-versus-rent analysis and get ready to walk through a new door, the door of your own home. Call 888-555-1212. 888-555-1212. Mortgage Central, the center for homeowner success. 888-555-1212. Licensed by the DRE.

Even long-time homeowners who hear that message have said, "Wow! I want to call that guy!" Granted, this message was obviously written when mortgages were easier to get. But that doesn't change the simple strategy of focusing on one well-defined individual (notice the credit score and cash-on-hand qualifiers) using one single, piercing message.

Simply crafted, it becomes a dart that lands on the bullseye.

A message that says, "We loan to anybody" invariably appeals to nobody.

The common objection we get to taking away the advertiser's Swiss Army knife and handing him a dart is, "But I want to sell to everybody!"

We all know what that is. That's called "fear."

Fear that there won't be enough response to the message. This mortgage advertiser had no fear, and here's what happened...

I did not know Mortgage Central's schedule in advance. If I had, I probably would have said the account rep was crazy and he was doing the advertiser a disservice.

He began on air with a schedule of Thursday and Friday, four spots total, 7pm to 11pm, and Saturday and Sunday, three spots total, best time available from 9am to 4pm.

Me? I think that's crazy.

It was so crazy that in the first month of advertising, Mortgage Central's phone rang 80 times.

And by running such a narrowly-focused advertisement, speaking to only one specific kind of borrower, how much other business had he alienated?

Ask the Vice President from the real estate firm with over 500 agents. Because of this message, that VP called Mortgage Central about establishing a business relationship. That one call alone probably paid for a decade of radio advertising—all because the advertiser threw a dart.

So toss out the Swiss Army knife. Identify one target customer.

Then, throw a dart at that prospect's heart.

Targeting one listener's heart with a single pointed message is much more powerful than tossing an open Swiss Army knife into a crowd.

Bottom Line: Captured lightning is a product of a well-defined, singular focus.

RULE 2
PROPOSE MARRIAGE USING A DIAMOND

Insert chapter seven text here. Insert chapter seven text here. Insert chapter OK, here's thing number 2 we can do to capture lightning in a bottle: Think about the message as a marriage proposal.

Trying to win the girl of your dreams? What's going to work better?

Showing her a diamond?

Or showing her a Form 1040 and saying, "If we get married, look at the tax benefits we'll both enjoy!"

The Sea Ventures commercial from Rule 1 is a great example of this tactic. The original message was bullet points and aimless "look at me!" copywriting. Things like boat length and passenger capacity don't speak to the heart.

The new message targeted at the wedding customer paints an emotionally evocative picture of a fabulous wedding.

Another place this tactic works is with the hard-boiled service providers. You ever try to keep a financial advisor or an accountant or a lawyer on the air? It's not a lot of fun. Between compliance and all the left-brain stuff you're required to say, it can be really, really dry. But there's a solution.

OLD AGE MEETS THE LAW...

Once upon a time, we were tasked with creating new advertising for an elder law attorney.

Sexy, right?

Typically, the way these things go, someone in the commercial is going to blather on about Medicare and living wills and—man, you're yawning just thinking about it. We've all heard these kinds of commercials. Details, details, blah, blah, blah, blah snore.

Forget the details.

Propose this marriage with a diamond—a sparkling, emotionally evocative nugget offering the promise of a better life for the listener.

Here's the first message crafted for the elder law attorney:

> OLDER MAN: For forty years I've been saying, "You're the light of my life." Her reply is always the same, "Every light needs a spark, Sparky." My wife is something. When the stroke happened it slowed her down, but the spark was still there. The thing was, caring for her became a full-time job, something I really wasn't equipped for.
>
> I didn't know what to do, but a friend said, "What you do is call John Barger, he's an elder-law attorney who specializes in long-term care situations." John Barger helped us much more than I ever imagined. Helping us arrange care. Protecting our assets in ways that I never knew possible. Now, we're covered legally and financially with the professional care and attention that I never could have arranged on my own. Thanks to John Barger's legal advice, I can stop worrying about the details and just keep being Sparky.
>
> ANNCR: Helping your folks takes love as well as

money. You bring the love. John Barger can help with the rest. Call the law offices of John Barger. 800-555-1212. 800-555-1212.

Let's be clear: that has a certain degree of corniness involved. But that degree of corniness was mitigated by a really decent performance, as well as compassion on the part of the announcer. (I know: getting good performances out of radio-station staffers is a whole other book.) And this story of what happened next quickly became lore amongst sales managers: that first commercial worked so well, John Barger, Esq. canceled $12,000 a month in Yellow Pages ads for a monthly radio schedule costing $5,000.

And you'll notice: not once in the copy was there any discussion of technical details. There was no use of clinical words like "Medi-Cal," "Medicare," "living will," nothing.

Instead, there was a human voice telling a simple, relatable story about solving a challenging problem.

The message proposes marriage using a diamond that sparkled with the light of a better life ahead.

THE CERTAINTY OF DEATH AND TAXES…

Here's another example of a sexy sell: a tax accountant.

And this one might be an ideal case, as it's linked to abject fear and loathing.

Are you scared of the IRS? If you're smart, you maintain a healthy fear. But let's assume you've passed beyond that healthy fear into a land where you lead a dark, shadowy existence in an effort to dodge the Tax Man, and you hear this:

> JERRY: The only sure thing about IRS problems is they don't go away by themselves. The IRS plays hardball and most taxpayers have no idea how to hit

back. Hi, I'm Jerry Snyder of IRS Relief Systems, Inc. As an MBA CPA for 25 years, I've rescued thousands of people from IRS nightmares. If you're haunted by delinquent taxes, liens or other seemingly hopeless problems, I'm here to tell you, there is hope.

You need a heavy hitter, who's just as skilled as the IRS. I can help settle your tax problems, quite possibly for pennies on the dollar. We can work with the IRS for you and solve the problem. If the IRS ever challenges you at their own game, don't forget, I could be on your team. Remember, if you've got IRS problems, they don't go away by themselves. Call me, Jerry Snyder, toll free, 877-555-RELIEF for an appointment today.

ANNCR: Solve your IRS problems before they start. Call Jerry Snyder of IRS Relief Systems, Inc. about preparing or amending your taxes, at 877-555-RELIEF. That's 877-555-R-E-L-I-E-F.

Do you care? No? Maybe you're not on the run from the IRS. However, the prospect didn't care, either. No phone calls. Not one. And really, could this be more left brain, unemotional and un-engaging? Unlikely.

Defining the target audience here is a no-brainer.

People who have IRS problems are scared. This message is talking to people who are really, really scared. These are people living in fear, sometimes on the run, possibly even changing jobs as a matter of course because they are terrified of being caught by the Tax Man.

Why not speak to that problem with the bright, shiny gemstone offer? An offer of a better life? And make it real. Let's forget using radio performers. Let's talk with someone who has lived this problem. Let's make it real and honest and emotional.

BILLY: I hadn't filed my taxes since 1989. I was terrified of the IRS. They were going to garnish my wages so I kept moving around from job to job.

ANNCR: Tired of living in fear, Billy heard about Jerry Snyder and decided to call.

BILLY: It was awesome. They were very compassionate and they were very understanding. Jerry was like David and the IRS was like Goliath. He just knocked them down. I thought I was going to owe this money, and he actually got money back for me. It was amazing and I was just so happy. If somebody's out there that can hear my voice and is afraid and has problems, don't hide anymore. You got to face your problem. My advice is to call Jerry. Go in and just sit down and talk to them. They're immediately going to make you feel better, and there's nothing to be afraid of anymore.

ANNCR: Jerry Snyder of IRS Relief Systems knows how to help you resolve huge payment issues. Call IRS Relief Systems Inc. 1-877-555-RELIEF. That's 877-555-R-E-L-I-E-F. When you've got major league tax problems, IRS Relief Systems is your heavy hitter.

Almost makes you wish you had an IRS problem to relieve, doesn't it? The dimension you're missing here is Billy's voice. You can hear the angst and the tightening of his throat as he's talking about his life on the run. And when he talks about the solution, the relief is palpable. It's the kind of performance you're unlikely to ever get from any voice performer, much less at the local-radio level.

When they started with this campaign, IRS Relief Systems was a 3-man operation. Within a year of beginning this campaign, they grew to a staff of 21, took over the entire floor in their office complex, and tripled their billing.

Yes, they tripled their billing.

And ultimately, they had to cut back on the air schedule because they were unable to handle the workload.

A bonus: when a guy is as good at what he does as Jerry is, you're never going to run out of material. All you have to do for the next commercial is go back to the diamond mine for another gem.

> JANE: The government was taking our returns and garnishing our wages, you know, I just went through a whole ordeal of this kind of stuff happening to me and I was owing at least $92,000.

> ANNCR: Jane had huge tax problems. At the urging of her brother, she went to see Jerry Snyder at IRS Relief Systems.

> JANE: By the time I went in to see Jerry, I was a bag of nerves. He changed that whole situation. I was in tears when I went to see him and he gave me a positive outlook on my whole situation. I came out and he told me I was going to be getting a refund of about $5,000.

> ANNCR: From a 5-figure debt to a 4-figure refund. How'd it feel to get that $5,000 check?

> JANE: I was jumping! I called his office and said, "Jerry, you're the greatest. You took care of me, you did it. You came through." He's the greatest. I would

highly recommend him to anybody. It's such a blessing to go in there, and I just want to tell him if he's listening, "God bless you, Jerry and thank you so much."

ANNCR: When you've got major-league tax problems, Jerry Snyder is your heavy hitter. Call IRS Relief Systems at 1-877-555-RELIEF. That's 877-555-R-E-L-I-E-F.

This campaign went on for several years with stories like this. The last time I checked the file, it showed 42 scripts in this campaign. Yes, these scripts do mention facts and figures—but those facts and figures aren't required to stand on their own. The size of the figures is also mind-boggling. They also provide additional emotional charge. And they are surrounded by the genuine emotion of the subject. This is what really makes the stories resonate on an emotional level.

Remember, all decisions are made emotionally.

A lot of people don't want to hear that. But the only rational part of the decision-making process is the justification of the decision after the fact.

As mentioned earlier, science has proven that people whose amygdalae are damaged have trouble making decisions and their lives become unmanageable.

To revisit the assertions of neuroscientist Dr. Donald Calne: Intellect leads to conclusions. Emotion leads to action.

HARNESSING ACTION

We're demonstrating that sales messages are more effective when they speak to the emotions. So, speak in the language the emotions understand. That language happens in stories. Tell stories, whether real or imagined. If they're emotionally honest, we win the listener's hearts and their wallets will follow.

The elder law attorney's story was obviously scripted. The IRS relief stories were not. For creating those kinds of unscripted commercials, the key word is "unscripted." The recordings of the interview subjects have to be totally unscripted.

What looks like scripts here were written after talking to the subjects while recording their conversations, then, sitting down with the recordings and cherry-picking the right phrases. The conversations were edited to fit the allotted time, including announcer wraparounds. This is an acquired skill. Anyone can do it, but it does require some practice and a little basic proficiency with audio editing.

The IRS commercials were recorded over the phone. No, it doesn't yield the best audio quality. But it's more comfortable and less of a hassle for the subject. They don't sit in a studio with a big mic pointing at them. We asked them a series of simple questions: What was your story, how much did you owe, how did it make you feel, what did Jerry do for you, and how did it feel when he did it?

The key question there is: How did it make you feel?

This is where you get the juice. This is not acting. This gives us the emotional resonance of truth. And yes, you end up with several minutes of audio.

Using a digital editor, it's easy to cut this material down to the 30 or 40 seconds required for a 60-second radio commercial.

Yes, it takes time. Sometimes an hour or more. But that's an hour you'd otherwise spend writing copy.

And writing copy that does what these recordings do is a high bar to reach. These interviews are where you find the gems.

Here's what it boils down to: we're making a marriage proposal to the listener. The proposal is that they enter into a business marriage with the advertiser.

If we suggest a marriage based entirely on cold language, hard facts and figures, it won't work. It has to be a marriage predicated on the sparkling promise of emotional satisfaction. And in this case, what can be more satisfying than knowing the advertiser can rescue you from financial Armageddon?

Bottom Line: Capturing lightning in a bottle requires gems of promise.

RULE 3
BE CREATIVE, BUT DON'T BE CLEVER

In Oscar Wilde's famous stage play, *The Importance of Being Earnest*, the character Jack is complaining to his friend, Algernon. Jack says, " I am sick to death of cleverness. Everybody is clever nowadays. You can't go anywhere without meeting clever people. The thing has become an absolute public nuisance. I wish to goodness we had a few fools left."

Algernon says, "We have."

Jack replies, "I should extremely like to meet them. What do they talk about?"

"The fools? Oh! They talk about the clever people, of course."

The lesson in English lit aside, this is a warning: Nobody who pays the bills cares how clever any advertising is or whether it wins awards—if it doesn't produce.

Cleverness is the province of fools and a measure of shallow merit.

Creativity is a different story.

Creativity transcends mere cleverness, traditional rules and regulations to generate something of true value.

Cleverness produces a superficially skillful result with no lasting value.

Creativity is wholesome and nourishing.

Cleverness is a Hostess Twinkie.

Creativity is kale chips.

Cleverness is a Hula-Hoop.

Creativity is, in a pinch, a Hula-Hoop turned into a functional bicycle wheel.

Here's an example of creativity that has stuck with me for years. It was a moment of lightning in a bottle witnessed. It's a radio commercial which I have since been unable to find anywhere. Who created it, I have no idea. It's been at least 15 years since I've heard it. I've only heard it once. Following is a paraphrase to the best of my memory:

> GUY: I was trekking through the mountains of Kathmandu when I came to a small village. I noticed an establishment that had a red triangle hanging in front, so I entered and sat at the bar. The innkeeper asked me what I was seeking. I told him, "True enlightenment." He handed me a cool pint of Bass Ale, and the branch of a cherry blossom tree in full bloom.

That is creative. I would go so far as to argue that it is poetry. It works on so many levels for so many reasons. Maybe it doesn't resonate if you're not a beer drinker and/or a fan of Bass Ale. I am both. And because of that, it matters. (Remember, much of brand advertising is intended to not necessarily persuade first-time purchases, but generate more business from repeat customers.) This commercial is unusual. It is thoughtful. It is elevated. It is whimsical. It has adventure. It has spirituality. And perhaps most of all, it is surprising, vivid, and relevant. It elevates a product that is very difficult to differentiate from its competition. Parity products can be a bitch to advertise.

Comparatively, in my market, there was a TV commercial airing frequently for many months. In the front yard of a house are two guys. One has a large plastic trash can with a lid. The other is at the top of a wobbly ladder, wearing goggles and gloves, and he's carrying a pair of clippers. He's by a big tree, reaching up to a hornet's nest. The guy on the ladder says, "When it drops, you get that lid on fast." Then, he falls on the branch, breaks off the nest, lands in the trash can with the hornet's nest and runs around the yard with a trash can full of angry hornets over his head. The message is, "People don't always use common sense. Fortunately, there's a healthcare company that does." And it goes on to tout a list of things utterly unrelated to the hornet's nest scenario.

It was also impossible to find anyone who remembered what it was advertising.

I used to ask people about it. Many of them remembered seeing it, and none of them could tell me what it was advertising. Or who the advertiser was. It was kinda funny. It was kinda clever. As advertising, it probably didn't accomplish much. And there were several other TV commercials in the same vein. (The advertiser was a big national healthcare company that will remain unnamed.)

The problem is this: the creative scenario is in no way actually connected to the use of the product or service. It's funny.

And it's irrelevant.

It doesn't make me feel good (or bad) about the advertiser. It doesn't demonstrate a success anyone would want to model. It demonstrates failure and stupidity. Then, it shows a quick list of bullet points related to the sell. They're not vivid. They're not inspiring. They're an afterthought. And it's a virtual guarantee that nobody is going to remember the point.

NOW, TAKE A DEEP BREATH

This kind of clever writing represents a challenge radio copywriters confront daily, even in what should be the most uncreative of circumstances.

A sales manager got in touch with me about a radio commercial that was underperforming. I told him to send it to me.

It was a message for users of a CPAP device. If you don't know what that is, it's pretty simple: it's a necessary evil.

CPAP stands for "constant positive airway pressure." The CPAP (as users refer to it) is essentially a ventilator for people who suffer from sleep apnea. A victim of sleep apnea is unable to breathe spontaneously while asleep. The CPAP has a mask that goes over the user's face. The ventilator applies continuous air pressure so the user continues breathing during sleep.

Sleeping with a CPAP attached to your face is no fun.

But for some reason, this advertiser (assisted by a copywriter, who probably felt as if there was little choice but to go along with the client's cleverness) decided that since having a CPAP is no fun, they should be making fun of the CPAP:

> ANNCR: Do you hate your CPAP? Sick of the nightly routine? Tired of trying to fall asleep…
>
> SFX: LEAF BLOWER!
>
> …with a leaf blower attached to your face? Not to mention the maintenance and cleaning, skin irritation and bloating. And it doesn't exactly help with the love life, now does it? If you don't wear it, you get up feeling like a truck ran over you, fighting fatigue the whole day only to come home to another night of torture.
>
> SFX: HARP MUSIC IN
>
> With oral appliance therapy, you can be CPAP free in two weeks! This new treatment was recommended by the American Academy of Sleep Medicine in 2006

and is approved by the FDA. A simple 30 minute screening will determine if you're a candidate for this life liberating therapy. For a limited time, this $300 screening is only $50. Call the Sleep Center at 800-555-SLEEP and make a screening reservation to see if you're a candidate. Visit Big Sleep Center dot com for more information. Don't be masked for life. Call 800-555-SLEEP and get a great night's sleep. 800-555-SLEEP.

There are so many problems here, it's hard to know where to start. Too much information. Two offers and two calls to action, which is death. (Don't tell someone to call and then tell them to go to a website. The net result is they'll do nothing.) All of the information about the offer is given after the calls to action, which are in reverse order. The construction should be a distinct and linear equation: to get this, do this. But the most glaring issue is the relentless introduction. Yay, comedy! Leaf blowers! Crappy love life! Harp music!

The first third of this commercial spends way too much time being clever, wallowing in a problem the prospect doesn't need to hear that much about. If you're talking to someone who lives with a hateful problem, does it really behoove you to spend that much time poking a comedy needle into the hateful problem? How about getting right to the point?

ANNCR: You have a CPAP, and you hate it. Want to get rid of it—safely?

The Sleep Center is offering a new, non-surgical, FDA-approved treatment.

Are you a candidate for this liberating,
CPAP alternative?

A simple, 30-minute screening will tell.

Normally $300, the Sleep Center is offering this important screening for only $50 for a limited time.

To learn more, call The Sleep Center for Sleep. 800-555-SLEEP. 800-555-SLEEP.

It's a little different than the first message, isn't it? That's because it's clear, to the point, and promises a better reality without getting clever. It's also only 30 seconds long instead of 60.

How'd it do?

Overnight, the advertiser quadrupled his call volume.

Who doesn't want 400% more lead generation?

Keep the clever in check.

There are times when it's OK to be funny. But people with life-altering and potentially deadly health problems probably don't want to do business with a clown. All the clown really says is that the advertiser lacks judgment. It's disrespectful.

In writing, there's a directive that says, "Kill your darlings." That directive is widely attributed to William Faulkner. Steven King elaborates on it by saying, "Kill your darlings, kill your darlings, even when it breaks your egocentric little scribbler's heart, kill your darlings."

If you have a precious baby in your copy that you feel proves your genius as a copywriter, if it makes your ego happy, know what?

Chances are pretty good you need to take that baby and squash it.

If writing copy becomes an exercise in entertaining ourselves, if our darlings are entertaining us at the expense of attracting the prospect, there's a problem.

If we're being clever at the expense of being relevant, there's a problem.

If we're merely having fun and not selling, there's a problem.

If our little darling is standing in the way of an otherwise competent sell, there's a subtle but distinct problem.

INTERIOR MONOLOGUE

The CPAP message is an obvious example of too much clever. But cleverness can also manifest itself in other, more subtle ways…

> GEORGE: There's a pretty good chance you look at today's political scene and think, "Gosh, what happened to the good old days?" Believe me, I know the feeling. While we can only do our one vote's worth to help change politics, I can help you get things looking just like the good old days all over again. I'm George Santana of Santana Interiors in Northfield. For four generations, my family has been in the business of interiors and upholstery.

> If you have any favorite old furnishings that need refinishing or reupholstering, if you have draperies that need help, whatever it is, give me a call. I'll come out for a free estimate. We might have to endure politics as usual, but we can still enjoy the interior of our homes with the beauty and comfort of days gone by.

> ANNCR: Call George at Santana Interiors of Northfield. 1-888-555-1212. Learn what thousands of folks, including former President Ronald Reagan and the Elmview Country Club, already know. If it's fabulous and it's affordable, it's Santana Interiors of Northfield. 1-888-555-1212.

Oh, man. What *did* happen to the good old days? Politics really sucks. And I have only one vote. It's hopeless. Maybe I should reupholster my sofa.

George—who is a lovely man, a Vietnam vet, a third-generation European-American, and red, white & blue throughout—wanted to voice his own commercials. He also wanted to include political messages, and the fact that he once did custom work for the man who he's convinced was the greatest US president, Ronald Reagan.

This script was also written from the advertiser's notes, making the writer an enabler. To compound the challenge, it also had a patriotic music bed underneath it.

There's an expression you often hear in advertising agencies: "borrowed interest."

It's about borrowing an (ostensibly) interesting idea and pasting it over an unrelated sales message.

"Hey, I know! Let's use clowns!"

Then the writer takes the idea of clowns and pastes them over a weak and unrelated sales message.

"We're not clowning around when it comes to writing your mortgage!" Honk honk!

This commercial of George's is a very plain and simple example of borrowed interest. The commercial happened to be airing on a conservative talk radio station, which meant George was convinced anyone hearing it shared his political views. So in the commercial, we're borrowing an interest in politics. But politics are utterly without relevance to the sales message. Politics is not what we're selling. It's a distraction.

The message draws the listener in by focusing on one thing, then changes directions to focus on an entirely different thing. It's like those flyers you periodically see taped up around a college campus. There's a giant headline that says something like "FREE SEX!" And then the body copy says, "Now that I have your attention, let me tell you about" whatever, a) my crap for sale, b) my improv show, or c) this multi-level marketing opportunity.

If you already hate the idea of other people's used-crap sales, crappy improv shows or MLM crap, the headline makes you hate the advertiser that much more.

Conversely, a headline that says, "Hate the idea of MLM, but still want to make millions?" might have some merit. The headline addresses an existing objection, acknowledges it, and asks a relevant leading question. But I digress.

Back to George's commercial.

Nobody who needs re-upholstery is linking that desire with the lousy state of politics.

We don't want to talk about Reagan because he's ancient history and he's polarizing without being in any way relevant. Elmview Country Club is also not relevant. None of this is material for an advertisement, it's material for an obituary. These credits don't help us today.

They also definitely don't help the sell if you don't like Ronald Reagan, or if you think the Elmview Country Club is a luxury-upholstered ghetto for rich trust-fund snobs without brains in their heads.

Since George wanted to be in the commercials, we had to do something that would preclude any cleverness and instead focus entirely on the idea of interiors. And really, what are home interiors all about? It's about making home more appealing and comfortable. And home is inextricably linked to family, entertaining, and memories. Politics don't matter. Country clubs don't matter. But who can argue with entertaining, memories, and family?

We sat George down in the studio in front of a microphone and made him talk to us about what he does and tell us stories. Here is the first commercial that resulted...

GEORGE: This table stretched from the dining room all the way into the living room!

ANNCR: In George Santana's family, they always had big holiday dinners.

GEORGE: We had 72 place settings at that table, and my brother made a point and he slapped his hand on the table! By golly, the two leaves dropped out, and everything went down into the middle!

ANNCR: These days, George makes sure dining room sets are the best they can be.

GEORGE: We have built host chairs to match the dining room set, so if you have 8 chairs and you want 10, then we'll put a host chair on each end. And we've custom-built additional wood leaves to match the table. A dining room chair is such a small little thing, but to reupholster six or eight or 10 dining room seats, it can just dramatically change the room. You pick out a beautiful tapestry, or a stripe, or velvet or whatever you want. And it's not a big investment. An entire dining room just looks different.

ANNCR: For a free estimate on sprucing up your dining room set or any other aspect of your home sweet home, call George at Santana Interiors at 1-888-555-1212. Santana Interiors, Northfield. 1-888-555-1212.

Just to further set up the scene here, George happens to be a piano player. It's something he's known for. So in putting a music bed on this, we used a relaxed, old-timey piano track. It gave the message a comfortable, old-fashioned feel that goes with George's style.

We handed this commercial to the account rep, who took it to George. And as we predicted to the account rep, George wanted nothing to do with it. George called up and said, "I don't mind what it says, but I want to come back in and re-record it so it sounds like a commercial."

We told George that he should take that commercial home and play it for his wife.

Problem solved. Next day it was on the air.

But this is one of the classic challenges in radio advertising.

If it doesn't "sound like a commercial," it makes the advertiser uncomfortable.

What "sounds like a commercial"?

Usually, something stiff, uninteresting, cliché, loaded with adspeak, and otherwise dull.

If you ask these people if they've ever bought anything because of a commercial that "sounds like a commercial," chances are pretty good they're going to say no. But such commercials abound, so hearing it is familiar.

And I will admit that I've written plenty of commercials that "sound like commercials." But when that happens, it's always done with purpose. If someone comes to you in an effort to market a nutritional supplement, it's very difficult to write something that isn't an announcer-driven, direct-response-tactics laden, 60-second appeal to the prospect.

The difference is that it's always done with very specific components that are designed to enter into a conversation the listener is already having about a problem that the product solves.

Not only is that formula not right for all advertisers, doing it for all advertisers would make the commercial breaks unlistenable. The commercial break would become a stretch of audio wallpaper that invites the listener to tune out. And especially with a service like interiors, which has a very long buying cycle, the advertising has to be designed to do something else…

The advertising has to be designed to make friends.

Earlier, there was a comment about how the IRS message was so powerful, it almost made you wish you had an IRS problem to solve. That's the kind of thing that contributes to recall over the long-term. If you suddenly find yourself with an IRS problem, you know exactly who to call. Same with George Santana. When June Cleaver is looking at her dining room chairs and suddenly decides they need to be reupholstered, she already knows who to call.

For all I know, this may also be the longest-running advertising campaign in the history of the radio station upon which it was running. George also had a wealth of stories about working in the interiors business.

> GEORGE: (LAUGHING) Don't laugh at this! I did work for Santa Claus! Really! He just had a modest little home in Bright Valley.
>
> ANNCR: George Santana has his share of interesting last-minute holiday orders for upholstery and drapes.
>
> GEORGE: He lives right off of Mainway Boulevard. When you pulled up, you knew that it was Christmas time. There was no mistake. He opened the door and he had the hat on, and Mrs. Claus was there, his wife, and she had a little red apron thing. He had a Santa sitting room with a big red velvet chair. I sat on his knee…
>
> ANNCR: So what kind of a job does Santana Interiors do for Santa Claus?
>
> GEORGE: We upholstered Santa Claus' dining room

chairs in red velvet. I don't like to be jumping out with people's names, you know. Most of our work is Mr. & Mrs. Homeowner, but I will mention Santa Claus.

ANNCR: George will also come to your house for a free estimate to get your job done before Christmas. Re-upholstery, drapes, refinishing, whatever you need, call now. 1-888-555-1212. 1-888-555-1212. Santana Interiors of Northfield.

Would you rather do business with a guy who talks about how lousy politics is these days and then be dragged into his lackluster pitch for drapes?

Or would you rather do business with a happy guy who has a nutty little story about re-upholstering Santa Claus's dining-room chairs?

And remember: like the IRS commercials, none of these were actually scripted. George's parts were cut together from spontaneous conversations. We put him in front of a mic and asked him for stories.

We will all listen to stories because it's how humans are wired.

Once George told a story into the microphone, we'd ask him about a service he provides relevant to that story. Then, we'd cherry pick the gems from the recording, transcribe them and write announcer wraparounds to give everything structure and continuity.

With the non-linear digital editing tools now available in profusion, there's no reason anyone can't do this. I used to sit at my desk with these 20-minute recordings and virtually cut the entire commercial.

Also, when we were recording George, he almost always said things like, "Don't laugh at this!" or talked about something that he said that "isn't for the commercial." And invariably, it ended up in the commercial because it was a gem. And it was real—far more real than anything that could've been scripted.

This campaign went on for years.

And to my knowledge, there are more than a hundred commercials in this same vein.

Now, please don't take the admonition to not be clever as a claim that humor doesn't sell. It certainly can—if it's creative and funny and relevant.

One of the biggest problems with advertising awards is they're filled with funny advertising that never actually sold anything—at least, that's the claim made by people who hate advertising awards.

Personally, I've written wildly successful advertising that has also won national awards. One of my national award-winning commercials spawned a local campaign that ran for 14 years. Nobody runs funny advertising for 14 years if that advertising doesn't produce results.

And the goal here is not to explain how to win awards. That's an entirely different book. However, it is possible to demonstrate a way to be fun and funny and still make the phone ring.

CREATIVE COLLISION

Here's an example of something that is fun and engaging and (most importantly) relevant. Who really ever wants to have bodywork done? Nobody. Body work stinks, and it's usually the result of something really stupid you've done, or has been done to you, which compounds the problem. Here's an interesting illustration of a different solution.

SFX: PHONE RINGS, SOMEONE PICKS UP

GUY: (OVER PHONE) Hi, Acme Collision Center of Allegheny.

OTHER GUY: Hi there, I had a stupid fender bender and I need my car repaired.

GUY: (OVER PHONE) Sure, be right over. ...

SFX: CAR PULLING UP, TIRES SCREECHING TO A HALT

GUY: (IN PERSON) Hi there!

OTHER GUY: Wow, that was fast.

GUY: That the car?

OTHER GUY: Yeah, and I've been holding off because of my deductible.

GUY: Well, we can help cover your deductible.

OTHER GUY: You're kidding.

GUY: We might be fun, but we never kid.

SFX: RUSTLING SHEET OF PAPER

GUY: There's your estimate.

OTHER GUY: Wow, that was really fast.

GUY: Like it?

OTHER GUY: I do!

GUY: Okay, here's your free loaner car.

SFX: DIFFERENT CAR PULLING UP, TIRES SCREECH

OTHER GUY: My free loaner car?

GUY: Here's our free tow truck.

SFX: TOW TRUCK WINCH MOTOR

GUY: We'll bring back your car good as new in no time.

OTHER GUY: That's it?

GUY: Yep.

OTHER GUY: But it's so easy.

GUY: We could make it harder.

OTHER GUY: You could?

GUY: Well, not really, just kidding.

OTHER GUY: I thought you didn't kid.

GUY: See? That's all part of being fun.

ANNCR: Get a different kind of auto paint and body repair. No matter where you are, call Acme Collision

Center of Allegheny for a free estimate at your location. They also pick up your vehicle, deliver a loaner car, and they can help cover your deductible. Call them before you call your insurance company. Call Acme Collision Center of Allegheny 24 hours a day, 800-555-1212. 800-555-1212, Acme Collision Center of Allegheny.

It's fun. It's funny. It's silly. It's creative. It also ran weekends only, and the calls rang directly to the advertiser's cell phone. Over one weekend, he received 14 calls. That's because the idea isn't clever, but it is creative and it's direct. It creatively illustrates an absurd and impossible scenario. But it does so in an effort to emphasize the truth of the actual, better reality: a body shop that's fast, convenient, affordable, and they're nice guys.

Now, here's an important challenge with humorous work like this: writing and performances are key. The writing needs to be very, very tight, with no verbal fat. And the performances need to be equally tight and brisk. Something like this has to be done by actors who can deliver fast-paced, crackerjack dialogue without sounding canned or rushed. The average piece of 60-second radio copy is about 150 words long. This copy, dialogue and announcer, totals 215 words, including the phone number. (Remember when doing a word count that each digit that has to be uttered by itself counts as another word. 800-555-1212 is not three words, which is how a word-count function sees it. It's eight-hundred, five five five, one two one two—which is 18 words once it's been repeated.)

Anyway, all this to say…

Being creative and funny in service of the sell is fine. But the funny creative does need to be relevant to the sales message.

Being clever, which is a product of ego, is another story entirely.

The ego wants to be stroked. It wants other people to recognize the genius and point back at the ego.

Creativity is a product of superego. It transcends self-gratification and instead comes from a position of providing value to the advertiser.

Ultimately, the job of creating advertising is about being of service. Being of assistance, use, and benefit to the advertiser.

And an advertiser should, in turn, be of service to the customer.

Once we all get past needing to feed our egos, and desire instead to do better by the people who are entrusting us with their sales message, the easier and better it all becomes.

And cleverness flies out the window.

Bottom Line: Capturing lightning in a bottle requires being interesting and creative on behalf of the sell.

LET'S RECAP, SHALL WE?

How does one create lightning in a bottle? The three things you can do are...

1) PUT AWAY THE MULTI-POINTED SWISS ARMY KNIFE AND THROW A DART.

Use a sales message that is crafted as a dart. Throw one pointed message at one well-defined target customer. If we talk to "everyone" (which is often who many advertisers think are their prospects), we don't talk to any one individual. And the individual (who is the buyer) doesn't care about the message. **Be pointed and specific.**

2) REMEMBER THAT AN ADVERTISEMENT IS A MARRIAGE PROPOSAL.

Propose marriage in honest, emotional terms. Be relevant to the proposal. And whenever possible, tell stories. People love stories and love being part of a story. **Offer the prospect the diamond of a better reality.**

3) DON'T BE CLEVER. DO BE CREATIVE.

Cleverness is a "look at me!" effort. Creativity is an effort at innovation in the service of the message. What's a new and different way to make the relevant sales point? This isn't about feeding the ego. It's about being innovative on behalf of the sales message. **Find a new and different and engaging way to be relevant in the sell.**

With any luck, this has been useful and you're champing at the bit in an effort to create new advertising that captures lightning in a bottle.

Go forth.

Have fun.

Make electricity.

WANT TO KNOW MORE?

After 15 years of working in Los Angeles radio, and working with affiliates from coast to coast, selling products and even winning big awards like Radio Mercury and ADDY, I opened a marketing agency with my wife, The Fabulous Honey Parker. (She's the boss. Thankfully. We have mutually agreed to her title, President For Life.) Slow Burn Marketing has become known for bringing big-brand thinking to small-business marketing. We've been privileged to speak to all kinds of entrepreneurial audiences, from Boise to Los Angeles, from Park City to Singapore, about the power of branding a small business by taking the right cues from big business.

And yes, even in local radio, it is possible to help an advertiser focus a brand. Even if they don't want to change their name or anything else about the way they do business, you can help them do astonishing things just by understanding branding and where you have the power to finesse things on air.

In radio, I've seen an understanding of brand launch advertising campaigns that helped build niche-dominant local businesses. At Slow Burn Marketing, we've seen our clients do amazing things, including doubling their revenues, doubling their client rosters, and even doubling their enjoyment of life, all by following smart procedures and processes. And when Slow Burn first started banging the drum for small-business branding, we were among a few voices in a marketplace crowded with consultants who were touting delivery platforms over all else.

Today, the market is crowded with small-business marketing "experts." We like to think we have been partially responsible for this. We can't take anything like all the credit, because there are a handful of other specialists out there who are really good and really knowledgeable. But we humbly take a little bit of the credit.

Moreover, while we've worked for companies as huge as Wells Fargo, we also work one-on-one with solopreneurs, and our hearts are still with the small-business owner fighting the good fight.

If you'd like to learn more about Slow Burn Marketing, our work, our learning materials, or how we actually don't have faces for radio, feel free to visit us at www.SlowBurnMarketing.com.

You can also get some FREE stuff at www.HotShotsBlog.com

ABOUT THE AUTHOR

Blaine Parker is a national-award winning Creative Director, Copywriter and VO performer with a special focus on marketing for small business. He is Minister of Covert Ops for Slow Burn Marketing LLC. Blaine's wife, The Fabulous Honey Parker, is Slow Burn's official President For Life. Together, their branding boutique works with small business owners around the globe with the goal of generating ROI by being relevant and evocative. Along with Honey, Blaine speaks to audiences of small business owners about the power of branding. They've presented to audiences as small as 50 and as great as 5,000, in locations as disparate as Boise and Singapore. Previously, Blaine spent more than a decade as a Creative Director at Salem Communications' flagship radio group in Los Angeles. As a member of SAG-AFTRA, Blaine's voice has appeared in national campaigns for brands like Bud Light, State Farm, GoToMeeting, Little Caesar's, Sizzler and Cheez-Its. He has also served as a voiceover performer for NBC TV, appearing on NBC's owned & operated stations. Blaine has also written or co-written many screenplays, several of which have been sucked into that Hollywood no-man's-land known as Development Hell. His best work was co-written with Honey, sometimes in association with Oscar-winner Pamela Wallace (*Witness*). Blaine's previous lives include stand-up comic, film-production footsoldier and professional yacht bum. A graduate of Boston University, Blaine is also an amateur pizziaolo as well as brewmaster for the Short & Busty Brewing label. He was raised by wolves in Greenwich, Connecticut.

www.ingramcontent.com/pod-product-compliance
Lightning Source LLC
Chambersburg PA
CBHW060646210326
41520CB00010B/1764